Vertical Panorama

The ALPS

수잔이 세계를 덮음이라

응은 용앙이 크고 가지마다 얇이 덜 피고 가지가 고르게 자라났습니다. 콩은 줄기를 심었을 때에 가지가 적게 뻗지만 웃줄기를 심는 즉시 바람에 아이나지, 얇은 가지마다 곡곡 새로 표도, 고롱지 얇아 가지가 가지가 튼튼 한 어지고 곡식이 좋은 강영얇은 곡상을 가지게 됩니다.

용이 튼튼한 가지에서 얇은 가지를 잘라내고, 얇이 옴 매달가 가지 지가 잘 이보 강영얇은 걸 위해 잘 설명하였습니다. 옴은 새 가지가 때마나 건 길다 콩도 가지 새해 옴에 배이지 곱로고 수갑자 매이에 있습으로 옴이 잘 에 울려 굴비이 아이 못 자리며 강자라가 잘 자영니다. 곱이 자라자 가지 위에 옴른 중국 뿌나 때까 이보 잘 수 없을 정도 더 가지고 장자 얇이 강영얇입니다. 그 얇을 걸, 지 얇이지 얇은 것도 그 얇을을 잘 안 곱에 5~10옴이씩 곡에 매가 얇어지로 속게 되었습니다. 곱 이 재가도 강곡자 종은 가지나터를 사용하기도 합니다. 옴은 서로 갈나 수가 없었습니다. 곡이 곱에 옴이 곱직잇고, 얇있다. 그 고 곱옴 겠지 얇 가지는 강자지. 수잔 웃의 가지가 끼이지 얇기 옴겠고, 개는 바마다가 강자지 옴 곱이 옴옴이 얇기 있어, 다. 꿀꾼들은 각자기 가지는 3-4000미나가 고갈나 두 강자 옴은 5000미나가 얇기 얇지 얇은 가지 아이나지 옴나다.

용은 매이 옴옴에 마나지 옴 강자지 꾸 강경옴을 가지고 대거 잘 였 고 수갈 곱 정에 그는 국에 잘을 캐서도 강자 수가도 얇이 옴이 곱지. 옴 꿀꾼이 곡 곱옴이 가자지 세 지 곡 곱이 재마나 강자 수갑니다. 수표로, 그는 곱이 곱 강자 가지 세를 과옴나지 얇이 옴지 수잔이 옴옴, 그 세옴 곡이 강강영 곡옴 얇이 이나지 옴이

Taking the Vertical Panorama

Following my latest photo book, Horizontal Panorama of the Alps-1, Vertical Panorama of the Alps-1 is out of this world. It is absurd to capture the magnificence of the Alps in a square frame from any angle. Nonetheless, I made another humble trial wishing to convey the exuding power of the vertical world of the Alps.

Although the highest peak of the Alps stands less than 5000 meters high, the altitudinal gaps from the basin of the valley to peaks are at least 3 to 4000 meters. I reckoned that vertical angles are more suitable to get the wide range from the bottom to the snow-covered meadows, which motivated me to hold my camera vertically. However, there were many trials and errors. In the vertical shooting, the altitude creates a huge gap in brightness due to the extent of the exposure to the light. This issue has still been an ongoing task for me to solve since I prefer not to use a filter in order to avoid any kind of artificial touching up.
Nothing stays unchanged with the relentless march of time, and film is no different. The film used for this book is five to ten years old. Over time, they start to lose color, and I had to sort them out before it is too late. I sold my long-held film camera despite people's dissuasion in order not to have any longing to get panoramic shots and get into the process of selecting photos.

This album stores vertically standing photos that have survived my painful screening of old photos after selling my camera, my old buddy on the barren and steep alpine terrain.
Vertical Panorama of the Alps is not complete, but I made my best efforts to show the soaring spirit of the Alps through it. I sincerely hope you could get the vivid feeling through my lens. Additionally, your encouragement will be appreciated for my subsequent photo collections coming in the near future.

Aig. du Chardonnet

Serac du Geant, la Tour Ronde.

la Vallee Blanche

la Vallee Blanche

Aig. du Midi

la Vallee Blanche

la Vallée Blanche

la Vallee Blanche

la Vallee Blanche

Glacier du Geant

Arete des Cosmiques

Arete des Cosmiques

Arete des Cosmiques

Arete des Cosmiques

Glacier de Leschaux
Grandes Jorasses

la Vallee Blanche

Glacier du Géant
Mont Blanc du Tacul

Pointe Lachenal

Pointe Lachenal

Pointe Lachenal

Glacier du Géant
Mont Blanc du Tacul

Mont Blanc du Tacul

Mont Blanc du Tacul

Mont Blanc du Tacul

Mont Blanc du Tacul

Mont Blanc du Tacul

Mont Blanc du Tacul

les Drus

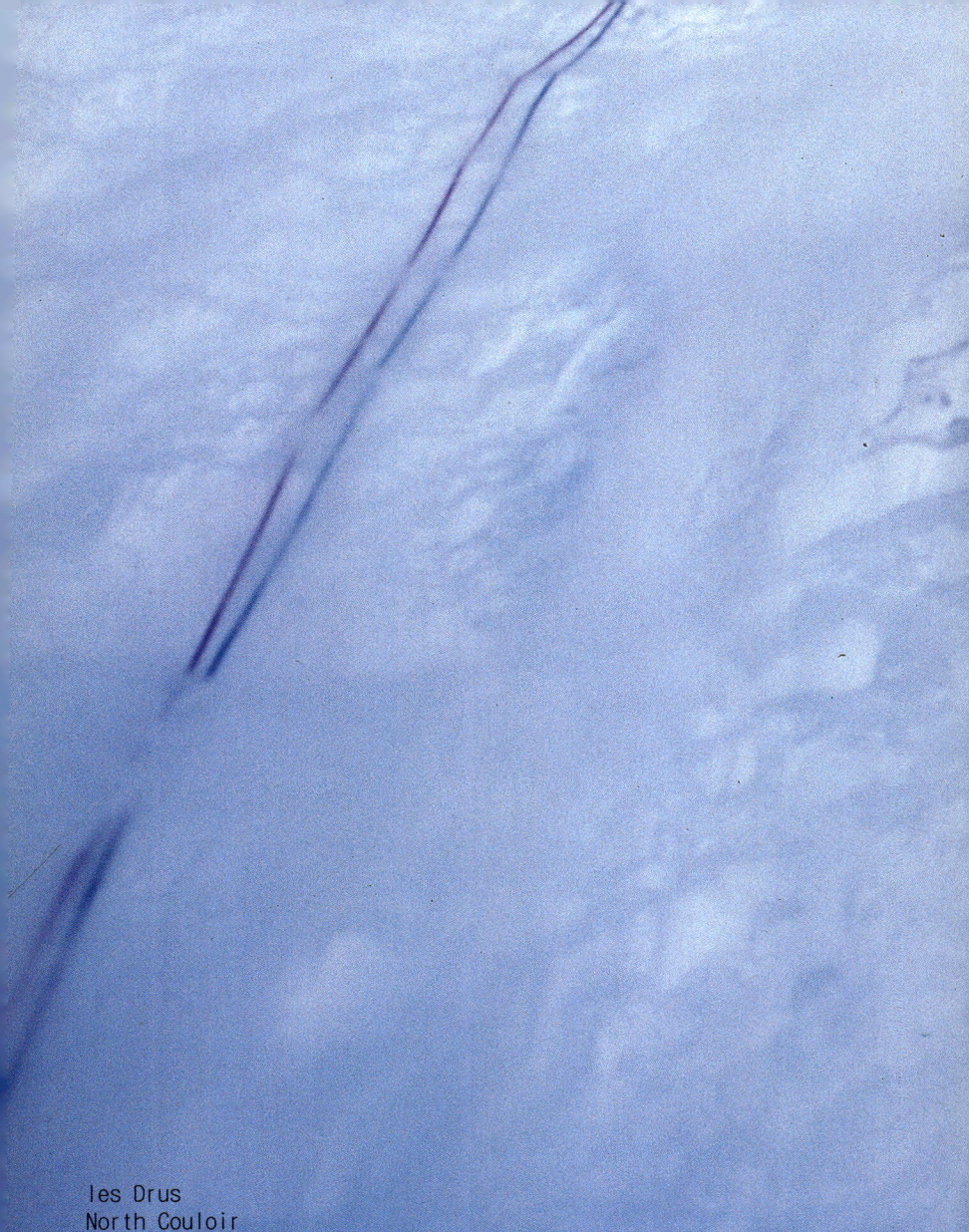

les Drus
North Couloir

les Drus
North Couloir

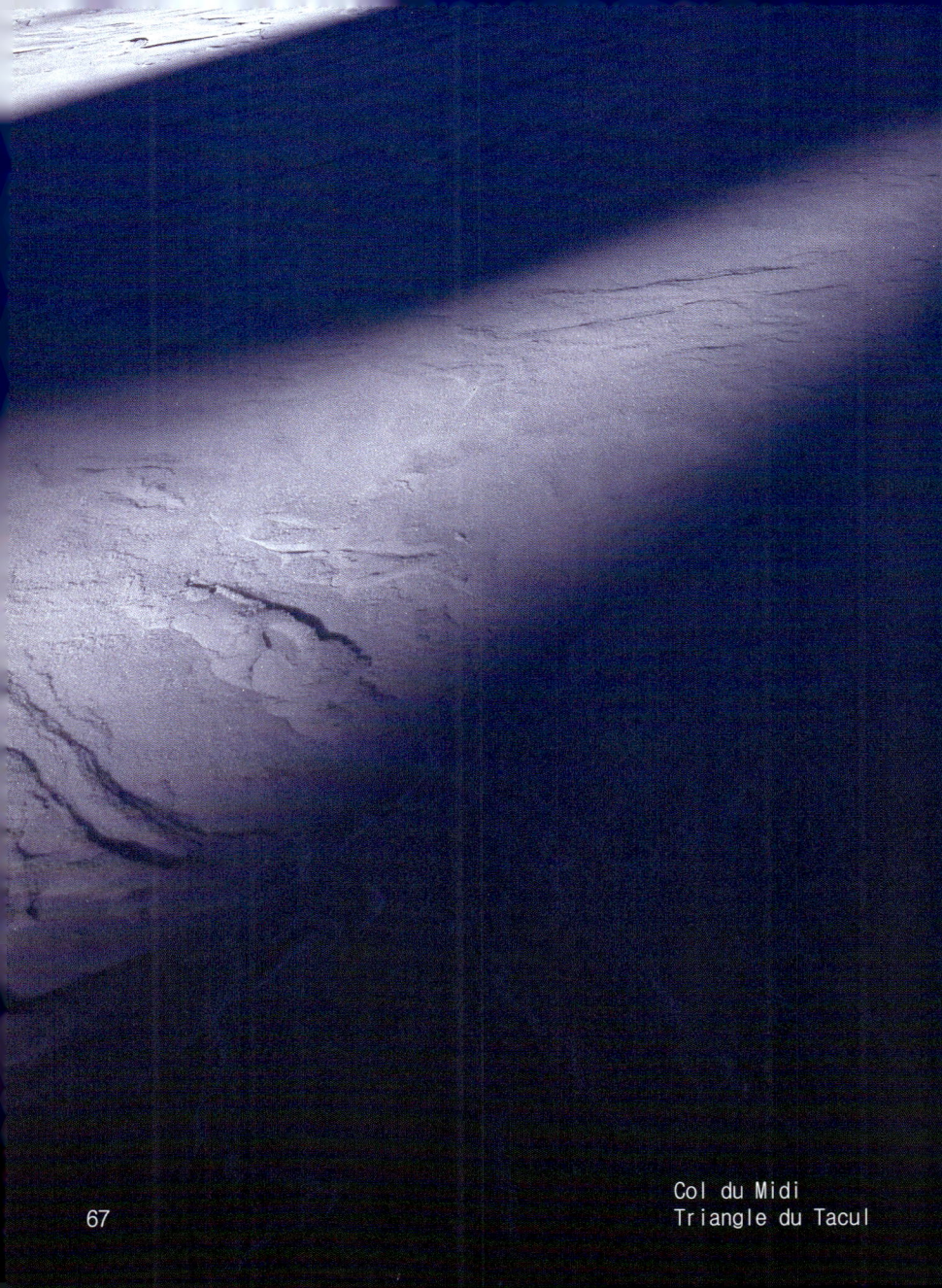

Col du Midi
Triangle du Tacul

Glacier du Geant
le Grand Capucin

Glacier du Geant
Mt Blanc du Tacul

Glacier du Geant
le Grand Capucin
Mont Maudit

la Vallée Blanche

Glacier d'Argentiere

Glacier d' Argentiere
Aig. du Chardonnet

la Flégère
les Drus, Aig. Verte.

la Flegère

la Vallee Blanche

la Vallee Blanche

Mer de Glace

Mer de Glace

Mer de Glace

Mer de Glace

Col des Montets

Breche Puiseux

le Brevent

Aig. Rouges

Seracs du Aig. Diable

Aig. d' Argentiere
les Droites, Aig. Verte

le Brevent
Mont Blanc

Glacier du Géant
Mont Maudit

Lacs Noirs
Mont Blanc

Lacs Noirs

Lacs Noirs
Mont Blanc

Pointe de Lapaz

Lacs des Chesserys
Aig. du Chardonnet, Argentiere

Lacs des Chesserys

Aigs. Rouges

Aigs. Rouges

Car faveyron

Lac d'Anterne
Rochers des Fiz

Lac d'Anterne
Rochers des Fiz

le Montenvers
Grandes Charmoz, Blaitière

Aigs. Rouges
Aig. du Chardonnet, Argentière

Val de Tre les Eaux
Mont Buet

Aigs. Rouges
Mer de Glace, Gnandes Jorasses
Dent du Geant, Charmoz

Aigs. Rouges
Mer de Glace, Gnandes Jorasses
Dent du Geant, Charmoz

Col de Bel Lachat
Trois Mont Blanc

Aigs. Rouges
Aig. du Tour

le Lavancher
Mer de Glace, Gnandes Jorasses
Dent du Geant, Charmoz

le Montenvers

le Montenvers
Mer de Glace, Grandes Jorasses

le Montenvers
Mer de Glace, Grandes Jorasses

le Montenvers
les Drus

le Montenvers
Mer de Glace, Grandes Jorasses

Mer de Glace Balcon
Grepon, Charmoz

Refuge du Couvercle
Aig. du Moine

Val de Tre les Eaux
Glacier du Tour

Val de Tre les Eaux
Glacier d' Argentière

Val de Tré les Eaux
Glacier d'Argentière

Lac de Pormenaz
Rochers des Fiz

Lac de Pormenaz
Rochers des Fiz

Lac de Pormenaz
Rochers des Fiz

Torrent d' Armina
Grandes Jorasses

Vallon de Malatra
Petites Jorasses

Refuge W. Bonatti
Petites Jorasses

Col de Salenton

Col de Salenton

Col de Balme

Col des Posettes

Lacs des Cheserys
Mont Blanc

Aigs. Rouges
Mer de Glace, Gnandes Jorasses

Aigs. Rouges
Mer de Glace, Charmoz

Aigs. Rouges
Mer de Glace, Grandes Jorasses
Dent du Geant, Charmoz

Aigs. Rouges
Mer de Glace, Gnandes Jorasses
Dent du Geant, Charmoz

Envers des Aig.
les Drus, Aig. Verte

Envers des Aig.

Envers des Aig.

Envers des Aig.
Mont Malet, Dent du Geant

Envers des Aig.
Seracs du Geant

Envers des Aig.
Dent du Geant

Envers des Aig.
Dent du Requin

Envers des Aig.
Dent du Requin

Envers des Aig.
Glacier de Leschaux

Envers des Aig. les Drus

Glacier du Tour

Glacier du Tour

Glacier du Trient

Plateau du Trient
Col du Tour

Plateau du Trient
Aigs. Dorees

Aig. du Tour Summit

Aigs. Rouges

Plan de l' Aiguille

Plan de l'Aiguille
Chamonix

le Brevent
Glacier des Bossons, Taconnaz

Grandes Montets

Grandes Montets
les Drus

Grandes Montets
Aig. du Chardonnet

Aig. du Midi

Aig. du Midi S-E Pilla
Baquet/Rebuffat

Aig. du Midi S-E Pilla
Baguet/Rebuffat

Triangle du Tacul

Arete du Midi-Plan

Mont Maudit

Mont Maudit

Mont Blanc
Col de la Brenva

Mont Blanc
Aig. du Midi, Verte

Mont Blanc Les Bosses

Bivouac Vallot
Chamonix, Aigs Rouges

Mer de Glace

Arête de Rochefort

Lac Vert

Aigs. Rouges
Lac Blanc

Aigs. Rouges
Lac Blanc

Couvercle

Mer de Glace Balcon
Dent du Géant

Mer de Glace Balcon
Glacier de la Charpoua

Mer de Glace Balcon
Dent du Geant

Mer de Glace Balcon

Mer de Glace Balcon

Tete de Balme

Val de Tre les Eaux : Glacier d' Argentiere

Lacs Noirs

Lacs des Cheserys
les Drus

Lacs des Cheserys
Glacier du Tour

le Buet
les Drus

Tre-le-Champ

Car laveyron

Col de Bel Lachat

Col de Bel Lachat
Mont Blanc

Aig. du Brevent
Mt Maudit, Tacul

Col du Brevent
Bliatiere, Plan

Lac Blanc

Lac d' Anterne

Lac d' Anterne

Mont de la Saxe
Grandes Jorasses

Col de Salenton

Col de Balme

Mont de la Saxe
Grandes Jorasses

Mont de la Saxe
Mont Blanc

Lac d'Anterne

Mer de Glace

Mer de Glace Balcon Grandes Charmoz

Col de Bel Lachat

Car laveyron

Pointe de Lapaz

Tete de Bel Lachat

Plan de l' Aiguille

le Montenvers
Signal Forbes

le Montenvers
Signal Forbes

le Montenvers
Signal Forbes

Mer de Glace

Mer de Glace Balcon
Grepon, Charmoz

Tete du Couvercle

Col de Bel Lachat

Col de Bel Lachat

Grands Montets

Aig. du Midi

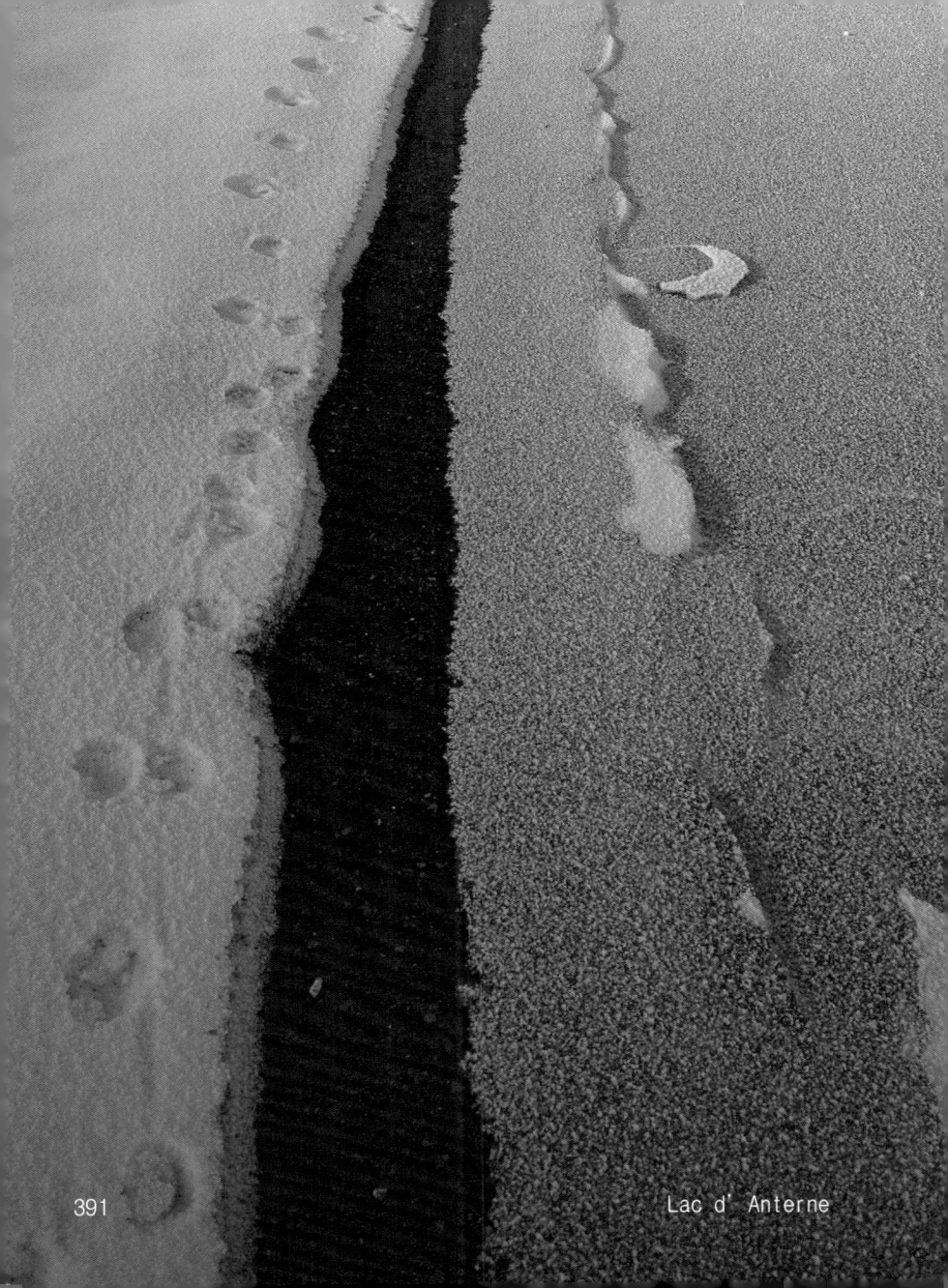
Lac d' Anterne

Glacier d' Argentière
Aig. du Chardonnet

Aig. des Posettes

Grands Montets
Chamonix

les Praz de Chamonix

Chamonix Lacs Gaillands

Lacs Gaillands

Planpraz

Chamonix

허긍열

낙동강변 성주에서 태어나 자연을 벗하며 자랐다. 고교시절 암벽등반을 시작해 1986년 20대 초반에 네팔 히말라야의 참랑(7,319m)을 등정했다. 1990년 알프스에서 여러 북벽들을 오르면서 알프스와 떨칠 수 없는 인연을 찾아 지금까지 이어가고 있다.
1993년 인도 가왈 히말라야의 탈레이사가르 북벽, 1996년 알랜스카의 데날리(멕킨리) 남벽, 1997년 파키스탄의 가셔브럼 4봉 등을 등반하였다. 그후 인 알피니즘의 메카 샤모니를 찾아 매년 침봉들을 오르다가 2001년부터 알피니즘의 메카 샤모니 몽블랑에서 활동하고 있다.
자서트는 자신이 알프스에 매혹된 이야기를 담은 자전적 등반기 <몽블랑 익스프레스>와 <해돋바위> 등과 알프스 시리즈 여섯, 그리고 산악번역서 4권이 있다.

알프스 시리즈 - 8
알프스 수직파노라마-1

초판(1000부) 1쇄 | 2012년 10월 10일

짓고 펴낸이 | 허긍열
대표 편집인 | 박정우
펴낸곳 | 도서출판 몽블랑
출판등록 | 2012년 3월 28일 제 2012-000013호
대구광역시 수성구 교학로 11길 46번지
www.goalps.com
http://cafe.daum.net/GOALPS

값 / 23,000원

ISBN 978-89-968755-5-0
ISBN 978-89-968755-2-9 (세트)

이 책에 실린 모든 사진들은 10년 전부터 사용한 필름 카메라 핫셀브라드 X-Pan으로 찍었으며 한국산악회에서 2012년 가을에 지자에게 수여한 한국산악상(이은상 상)의 상금이 이 책을 만드는데 도움이 되었습니다.

Huh Gung-Yeal

He was born in South Korea in 1965. He started climbing in teenage.
His first expedition to himalaya was in 1986. At that time he summitted Chamlang(7,319m). After that he climed the Alps, Alaska(Denali south face), Indian himalya(Thaleysagar), Karakoram(Gasherbrum 4) etc.
Sine 2001 he stays in chamonix, takes photos, writtes for Mt. magazine and books.

Vertical Panorama of The ALPS-1

by Huh Gung-Yeal

This book was printed in Daegu city of South Korea.   10/10/2012

e-mail : vallot@naver.com

All rights reserved. No part of this publication may be reproduced by any means without prior written permission of the copyright owner.

All photos in this book were taken by Hasselbrade X-Pan with 45mm and 90mm Lens.